God Can Heal Your Heart

MARIE SHROPSHIRE

HARVEST HOUSE PUBLISHERS
Eugene, Oregon 97402

GOD CAN HEAL YOUR HEART

Copyright © 1997 by Marie Shropshire
Published by Harvest House Publishers
Eugene, Oregon 97402

Library of Congress Cataloging-in-Publication Data

Shropshire, Marie
    God can heal your heart / Marie Shropshire.
        p.   cm.
    ISBN 1-56507-575-7
    1. Consolation.   2. Encouragement—Religious aspects—Christianity.
3. Hope—Religious aspects—Christianity.   4. Suffering—Religious
aspects—Christianity.   I. Title.
BV4905.2.S485   1997
242'.4—dc21   96-45431
                                               CIP

Printed in the United States of America.
97 98 99 00 01 02 03 /BF/ 10 9 8 7 6 5 4 3 2 1

I dedicate this book to all my friends and loved ones who
are hurting in any area of life.
You can be assured that God can heal your heart.
He has seen me through dark valleys.
He became light for me
when my path ahead looked foreboding.
He anointed me with His balm,
and soothed and healed my emotional bruises
as only He could do.
He gave me strength for my weaknesses
and comfort for my heartaches.
He provided for me when I wondered
where my provision would come from.
He replaced my inner turmoil with His peace.
He became my encourager in times of discouragement.
In Him I have found my identity and my joy.
What He did for me He can do for you.

Contents

From the Author

Much of this book was inspired by my experiences when I was passing through a dark valley. I have added many additional thoughts, hoping these will minister to your needs. I pray that this book will bring comfort and encouragement to you in your times of darkness and despair.

May you find, as I did, that when we encounter challenges along life's way, the Lord's presence is all we need at any given time.

Not for a moment do I claim that the words I've written are precisely God's words. But the words *were* divinely prompted. When we know the nature of God, we have a fairly clear idea of what He wants to say to us as His beloved children.

My prayer is that you will read these pages slowly and meditatively, and that you will see God more clearly as your ever-present Friend who is always true to His own nature.

I hope you will both read and meditate on the Scriptures provided at the end of each chapter. The more you meditate on such Scriptures, the more meaningful they can become.

—*Marie Shropshire*

Foreword

From the beginning of time, God has revealed His nature and character through His names. When He appeared in the burning bush and commissioned Moses to return to Egypt to lead His people out of bondage, Moses asked, "Whom shall I say sent me?" God replied, "I Am who I Am. Tell them I Am has sent you."

Such words may make little sense to most of us at first, but God was saying that He was real, self-existent, complete in Himself, and all-powerful. That is His nature and His name.

God is so great that heaven and earth cannot contain Him, so how can a mere name describe Him? Yet the more we know about the meaning of the various names used in the Bible to describe God, the better we understand God and His great love. The Hebrew and Greek languages were so much richer in meaning than our English language that a great deal of the original meaning was lost in translation.

Not every chapter title in this book gives a specific name of God, but each one reveals an aspect of the heart of God. When we better comprehend God's nature and character, we realize more fully that He is a God of love whom we can trust in our times of pain and distress.

I Am
Your Healer

*B*eloved one,
 I know the pain you feel.
 The anguish in your heart has been
 almost too much for you to bear.
 Your troubles are too great
 for you to understand.

*T*his is not a time for you
 to try to understand
 or to reason things out
 or to try to unravel the skein
 of your trying circumstances.

*I*ndulging in questions and reasonings
    will only make your trial more difficult
    and your inner pain more unbearable.
    To human understanding,
    some happenings have no reason.

*B*ut regardless of your afflictions,
    whether emotional or physical,
    I am the Lord who heals you.

*Y*ou have felt like a bruised reed
    and a flickering candle.
    I am the mender of bruised reeds
    and the restorer of dimly burning lights.

*M*y faithfulness will bring forth justice.
    You need not be discouraged.
    I comfort my people
    and have compassion on my afflicted ones.
    I bind up your wounds.

I took your infirmities
    and carried your sorrows.

By my wounds you shall be healed.
I was sent not only
to bring salvation to your soul
but to heal you
in every area of your being,
to make you whole.

I will accomplish my loving purpose
for you
and in you.
Trust me.
It shall be done.

Living Words of Scripture

I am the LORD who heals you (EXODUS 15:26).

I have seen his ways,
but I will heal him;
I will guide him
and restore comfort to him (ISAIAH 57:18).

*T*hen they cried to the LORD
      in their trouble,
      and he saved them from their distress.
      He sent forth his word
      and healed them (PSALM 107:19,20).

[*He*] forgives all your sins
      and heals all your diseases,
      [he] redeems your life from the pit
      and crowns you with love and
         compassion" (PSALM 103:3,4).

He himself bore our sins
      in his body on the tree,
      so that we might die to sins
      and live for righteousness;
      by his wounds you have been
         healed (1 PETER 2:24).

I Am
Your Strength

*D*ear broken child,
    I am aware of the weariness you feel.
    Your despair has weakened you.
    Your body is absorbing
    the overload of your mind,
    reminding you that
    you are spirit, soul, and body.

*Y*our brokenness calls you
    to greater integration
    of spirit, soul, and body.

I will strengthen you
in every area of your being.

My grace provides you
    with eternal encouragement
    and hope
    and vitality.
    I am faithful to provide you
    with strength,
    with protection.
    The trial will not be too much for you.
    I never put more on my children
    than they can bear.

As you rejoice in me,
    in spite of circumstances,
    your strength will return.
    Praise me,
    knowing that I am
    working out all things for your good.
    In quiet confidence
    you will find strength.

I will give you a new song.
You shall sing for joy
and be energized
as you become more aware
of my presence,
of my love.

*S*trength and joy are born
of a calm assurance of my promises.
So praise me,
delight in me.

*F*ace your future with me.
Feel my nearness.
Cultivate a sense of my joyful presence,
and draw from my strength.
"The joy of the Lord is your
strength" (NEHEMIAH 8:10).
Declare with David,
"For You are the God of my
strength" (PSALM 43:2 NKJV).

Living Words of Scripture

Splendor and majesty are before him;
> strength and joy in his dwelling
>> place (1 CHRONICLES 16:27).

The eyes of the LORD
> range throughout the earth
> to strengthen those
> whose hearts are fully committed
>> to him (2 CHRONICLES 16:9).

This is what the Sovereign LORD,
> the Holy One of Israel, says:
> "In repentance and rest is your salvation,
> in quietness and trust is your
>> strength"(ISAIAH 30:15).

The LORD gives strength to his people;
> the LORD blesses his people
>> with peace (PSALM 29:11).

O my Strength, I sing praise to you;
you, O God, are my fortress,
my loving God (PSALM 59:17).

I Am
Your Comforter

Grieving child,
   So often you have felt
   as the psalmist when he cried,
   "I am worn out calling for help. . . .
   I looked for sympathy,
   but there was none,
   for comforters,
   but I found none" (PSALM 69:3,20).

So few understand.
   Even fewer know how
   to comfort the hurting.

*B*ut I understand.

> I am the ultimate comforter.
> "As a mother comforts her child,
> so will I comfort you" (ISAIAH 66:13).
> Never hesitate to pour out your heart to me.
> Withhold not your thoughts.
> You will find help
> by putting your feelings into words.
> I will console you.

*D*o not withhold your tears.

> Tears promote healing.
> The day will come
> when I will wipe away all tears
> from the faces of my people
> once and for all.

*T*hat day is not yet.

> On this earth, tears are necessary.
> Never suppress them.
> Let them flow in my presence.

*D*o you remember that

> I was a man of sorrows

and acquainted with grief?
I understand sorrow
more than any human being.
My heart was touched
with the grief of Mary and Martha.
I wept when their brother Lazarus died.
I also comforted them.

My heart is touched with *your* grief.
    But that's not all.
    "I, even I, am he
    who comforts you" (ISAIAH 51:12).

Living Words
of Scripture

*P*raise be to the God and Father
    of our Lord Jesus Christ,
    the Father of compassion
    and the God of all comfort,
    who comforts us in all our troubles,

so that we can comfort
those in any trouble
with the comfort
we ourselves have received from God.
For just as the sufferings of Christ
flow over into our lives,
so also through Christ
our comfort overflows (2 CORINTHIANS 1:3-5).

As a father has compassion
on his children,
so the LORD has compassion
on those who fear him (PSALM 103:13).

My comfort in my suffering is this:
Your promise preserves my life (PSALM 119:50).

4

I Am
Your Light

$\mathscr{D}$ear one,
I have heard your prayers.
I am aware of your impression
that you're groping in darkness
without so much as a shaft of light
to direct you.

$\mathscr{D}$o not despair, dear one.
I am the light
in your darkness.

Do not look too much to others
for light at this time.
Look especially to me
and to the light
I have placed within you.

The darkness which seems to engulf you
cannot remain.
I am your light
as well as your salvation.
You need not fear.
Let me take your hand in mine
and lead you.
You will not stumble or fall.

Continue looking into my Word.
You will find comfort there.
The entrance of my words
will illumine your way.
My Word shall be a lamp to your feet
and a light for your path.

*T*he darkness will not continue
     to be dark to you;
     before too long, your night
     will shine like the day.
     You will see.

I came to be a light,
     not only the light of salvation
     but the light of comfort
     to troubled hearts.

*A*s surely as you received
     the light of salvation,
     you shall receive the light
     of my comfort.

I am the light of the world
     and I am your personal light.
     I will turn your darkness into light.

Living Words
of Scripture

The unfolding of your words gives light (Psalm 119:130).

You, O LORD, keep my lamp burning;
  my God turns my darkness into light (PSALM 18:28).

The LORD is my light and my salvation—
  whom shall I fear?
  The LORD is the stronghold of my life—
  of whom shall I be afraid? (PSALM 27:1).

Your word is a lamp to my feet
  and a light for my path (PSALM 119:105).

The people living in darkness
  have seen a great light;
  on those living in the land
  of the shadow of death
  a light has dawned (MATTHEW 4:16).

5

I Am Your Friend

$\mathcal{D}$ear lonely child,
  The one whom you expected
  to be your friend for life
  was incapable
  of enduring friendship.

$\mathcal{M}$any times close friends
  whom you thought you could trust
  will lift up their heel against you.
  It's sad but true.

But there is a Friend
who sticks closer
than a brother.

I am that Friend.
I will never fail you.
I will never betray your trust.
I am a Friend at all times.

You are my friend,
doing as I command.
I no longer call you
only a servant.
I call you my friend.

Others have persecuted you.
They first persecuted me.
My friendship reaches out to you
in perfect understanding.

Cling to me in these hours
of loneliness.

Abide secure in my love,
in my friendship.

I understand you through and through.
I know the extent of your loneliness.
I know the loss you feel.
I assure you
that you will experience gain.
No loss suffered with me
fails to result in gain.

G reater love
has no one than this,
that he lay down his life
for his friends (JOHN 15:13).

I have lain down my life for you.
How great is my love
for you, my friend!

W hen you especially need
to be reminded of my friendship
recall the words of this song:

What a Friend we have in Jesus,
All our sins and griefs to bear!
What a privilege to carry
Everything to God in prayer. . . .
Can we find a Friend so faithful,
Who will all our sorrows share?
Jesus knows our every weakness;
Take it to the Lord in prayer.
                    —*Joseph Scriven*

Living Words of Scripture

A friend loves at all times (PROVERBS 17:17).

*T*here is a friend
    who sticks closer than a brother (PROVERBS 18:24).

*Y*ou are my friends if you do what I command.
    I no longer call you servants,
    because a servant does not know

his master's business.

Instead, I have called you friends (JOHN 15:14,15).

*A*braham believed God,
    and it was credited to him
    as righteousness,
    and he was called God's friend (JAMES 2:23).

6

I Am Your Water of Life

Beloved one,
  I am conscious of your dryness.
  You feel as if
  you're trudging through
  an endless desert,
  and that you are one
  with the parched earth.
  Yes, you feel as dry as the parched ground.

You are thirsty for truth and life.
  But you have not understood
  that I am the Water of Life.

I am *your* Water of Life.
I know how you feel.
On the cross I felt lonely and thirsty.
I was thirsty and they gave me vinegar.
I suffered in your behalf
on the cross and
in my earth walk.

Because of my suffering,
        I am able to pour water
        on all who are thirsty.
        I give you living water;
        I am your Water of Life
        and hope
        and joy.

I am a spring of water
        welling up within you.
        The day will come
        when streams of living water
        will pour through you

to quench the thirst
of your fellow travelers.

*B*ut now, like the woman at the well,
you have not realized
that I give living water
to all who ask for it.
I said to that woman,
"If you knew the gift of God
and who it is that asks you for a drink,
you would have asked him
and he would have given you living
water" (JOHN 4:10).

I say to you as I said to her,
"Whoever drinks the water
I give him will never thirst.
Indeed, the water I give him
will become in him a spring of water
welling up to eternal
life" (JOHN 4:14).

You need not perform or keep any laws
    in order to receive this spiritual water
    in greater abundance than you have received.
    More of it is yours for the asking.
    Only believe it.

The woman at the well did not know me as Savior.
    You do.
    As your Water of Life,
    I am not only Savior
    but giver of abundant life.

You are my child,
    but you have not understood all that this
    entails.
    You will continue learning and
    experiencing my goodness and greatness.

For I will pour water on the thirsty land,
    and streams on the dry
    ground (ISAIAH 44:3).

*T*ry to grasp the metaphor in this passage.
>   Know that my love and concern for your
>   well-being are far greater than my concern
>   for the land.
>   As surely as I supply literal water
>   to the parched earth
>   I am able to supply you
>   with all the spiritual water you need.
>   "To him who is thirsty
>   I will give to drink without cost
>   from the spring of the water
>   of life" (REVELATION 21:6).
>   "Come, all you who are thirsty,
>   come to the waters" (ISAIAH 55:1).

*D*ear child, the day will come
>   when you will know the truth of these words:
>   "The LORD will guide you always;
>   he will satisfy your needs
>   in a sun-scorched land
>   and will strengthen your frame.

You will be like a well-watered garden,
like a spring whose waters never
fail" (ISAIAH 58:11).

I am indeed your Water of Life.

Living Words of Scripture

I provide water in the desert
and streams in the wasteland,
to give drink to my people,
my chosen (ISAIAH 43:20).

He leads me beside quiet waters
(PSALM 23:2).

He will be like rain
falling on a mown field,
like showers watering the earth
(PSALM 72:6).

*H*e waters the mountains
    from his upper chambers;
    the earth is satisfied
    by the fruit of his work
    (PSALM 104:13).

I tell you the truth,
    no one can enter the kingdom of God
    unless he is born of water and
        the Spirit (JOHN 3:5).

*T*he Spirit and the bride say, "Come!"
    And let him who hears say, "Come!"
    Whoever is thirsty, let him come;
    and whoever wishes,
    let him take the free gift
    of the water of life (REVELATION 22:17).

I will sprinkle clean water on you,
    and you will be clean;
    I will cleanse you
    from all your impurities. . . (EZEKIEL 36:25).

. . . Jesus stood
     and said in a loud voice,
     "If anyone is thirsty,
     let him come to me and drink.
     Whoever believes in me,
     as the Scripture has said,
     streams of living water
     will flow from within him" (JOHN 7:37,38).

As the deer pants for streams of water,
     so my soul pants for you, O God.
     My soul thirsts for God,
     for the living God (PSALM 42:1,2).

7

I Am
Your Provider

*B*eloved child,
    You have wondered
    how you would be provided for.
    I have ways and means
    that you know not of.

*E*ven those who are evil
    know how to give good things
    to their children.
    How much more will I, your Father,
    give to you all things
    needful for life and godliness.

Lean on me.
Continue to learn of me.
Trust in my great and precious promises.

I, who provided manna
for my children in the desert,
have not changed.
I am ever mindful
of the needs of my children.
My kindness goes on forever.
I, who have done great things for others,
will not fail you.

*A*ll who are hungry or thirsty
need only come to me.
Whether the need is spiritual
or material,
I am your provider;
I will supply.

I have made an everlasting covenant
with my people.

You, beloved one,
are included in that covenant.
No good thing do I withhold
from those whose walk is blameless.
Look to me,
and I will open doors for you.
I will bestow honor and favor upon you.

My storehouses are full;
You shall be satisfied with plenty.
Dwell not on your limitations
but on my provision.

Those who seek the Lord
lack no good thing (PSALM 34:10).

Living Words
of Scripture

Are not five sparrows sold for two pennies?
Yet not one of them is forgotten by God.

Indeed, the very hairs of your head
are all numbered.
Don't be afraid;
you are worth more than
many sparrows (LUKE 12:6,7).

Consider how the lilies grow.
They do not labor or spin.
Yet I tell you, not even Solomon
in all his splendor
was dressed like one of these.
If that is how God clothes
the grass of the field,
which is here today,
and tomorrow is thrown into the fire,
how much more will he
clothe you (LUKE 12:27,28).

God is able
to make all grace abound to you,
so that in all things at all times,
having all that you need,

you will abound in every
good work (2 CORINTHIANS 9:8).

My God will meet all your needs
according to his glorious riches
in Christ Jesus (PHILIPPIANS 4:19).

He who gives to the poor will lack
nothing (PROVERBS 28:27).

I know the plans I have for you,
declares the LORD,
"plans to prosper you
and not to harm you,
plans to give you hope and a
future" (JEREMIAH 29:11).

I will restore their fortunes
and have compassion on
them (JEREMIAH 33:26).

*Y*ou still the hunger of those you cherish;
    their sons have plenty,
    and they store up wealth for their
        children (PSALM 17:14).

*I*n times of disaster they will not wither;
    in days of famine they will enjoy plenty
    (PSALM 37:19).

8

I Am the Lifter
of Your Head

*D*ear one,

    During this time of your hurting
    the enemy wants to keep you down.
    But I live within you
    and am greater than he.
    I desire to lift you up.
    I am a shield around you
    and the lifter of your head.

*I*n the day of trouble

    I keep you safe.
    Let your heart be steadfast,

trusting in me.
Look up.
I am enthroned on high.

I will lift you from the ash heap.
Wait for me and
you will see my goodness.

S pend time out of doors
as often as you can.
See the beauty
in my creation.
Look away at the mountains.
Observe the trees,
tall and lofty.
Feel the grass under your feet.
Smell the fragrance in the air.
Listen to the water
gurgling in the streams.

L ook up at the beauty of the blue sky;
see the clouds
softly, gently floating by.

46

This is my world,
created for my pleasure
and for yours.

Look up and be reminded
of my power,
of my love.
Hear the birds singing.
See the loveliness of the flowers.

All these are expressions of my attributes.
And so are you.
I have made you only a little lower
than the heavenly beings.
I have crowned you
with glory and honor.

Rejoice in the majesty of my name,
knowing that all things are yours.
In due time you shall reap;
joy and gladness shall be yours.

Let your eyes ever be on me.
I will free you

from the snare of the enemy.
Put your hope in me
all the day long.
I am with you;
I am your Lord
and you are my child.

*D*eclare with the psalmist,
"You are a shield around me, O LORD,
my Glorious One,
who lifts up my head" (PSALM 3:3).

Living Words
of Scripture

*I*n the day of trouble
he will keep me safe in his dwelling;
he will hide me in the shelter
of his tabernacle
and set me high upon a rock.
Then my head will be exalted

above the enemies who surround me;
at his tabernacle
will I sacrifice with shouts of joy;
I will sing
and make music to the LORD (PSALM 27:5,6).

As for God,
his way is perfect;
the word of the LORD is flawless.
He is a shield
for all who take refuge in him (PSALM 18:30).

Blessed is the man
who makes the LORD his trust" (PSALM 40:4).

9

I Am Your

Peace

Beloved disturbed child,
    You have been churning with turmoil.
    Your circumstances have robbed you
    of your peace.
    The enemy comes
    to steal,
    and kill,
    and destroy.

But I came to give you
    abundant life
    and lasting peace.

In spite of your hurt,
>   you can receive abiding peace—
>   a peace deeper
>   than you have ever known.
>   I give supernatural peace.

The more time you spend with me,
>   knowing me
>   in a deeper dimension,
>   the greater will be your peace.

I never withhold my peace from you,
>   but you are able to receive
>   my peace in greater measure
>   when you dwell in my presence.

I will teach you
>   more about myself.
>   I will fill you with peace,
>   a peace that the world
>   cannot understand.

I keep those in perfect peace
>   whose minds are steadfast on me.

51

You will grow in your ability
to receive an abundance
of my peace.

*Y*ou have peace *with* God.
You received that
when you accepted my salvation.
You are now in a position
to become more receptive
to the peace *of* God.

*C*ultivate a consciousness
of my peace.
Peace is one of the most significant
words in the New Testament.
When you lie down at night,
say to yourself,
"I will lie down
and sleep in peace,
for you alone, O LORD,
make me dwell in safety" (PSALM 4:8).

When disturbing thoughts
        awaken you in the night,
        remind yourself that
        my peace,
        which is beyond
        human understanding,
        will guard your heart
        and your mind.

I am with you at all times
        to keep you safe,
        to fill your heart with peace.

My voice of peace is heard
        in my written Word.
        But my voice is more than Scripture.
        My voice speaks
        to your inner consciousness
        to flood you with peace.
        Indeed, I am your peace.

Living Words
of Scripture

The LORD gives strength to his people;
    the LORD blesses his people with
      peace (PSALM 29:11).

Seek peace and pursue it (PSALM 34:14).

The meek will inherit the land
    and enjoy great peace (PSALM 37:11).

I will listen
    to what God the LORD will say;
    he promises peace to his people,
    his saints (PSALM 85:8).

Great peace have they
    who love your law,
    and nothing can make them
      stumble (PSALM 119:165).

Do not be anxious about anything,
>   but in everything,
>   by prayer and petition,
>   with thanksgiving,
>   present your requests to God.
>   And the peace of God,
>   which transcends all understanding,
>   will guard your hearts
>   and your minds in Christ Jesus (PHILIPPIANS 4:6,7).

I will grant peace in the land,
>   and you will lie down
>   and no one will make you afraid (LEVITICUS 26:6).

Lord, you establish peace for us;
>   all that we have accomplished
>   you have done for us (ISAIAH 26:12).

This is what the LORD says:
>   "I will extend peace to her
>   like a river,

and the wealth of nations
like a flooding stream;
you will nurse
and be carried on her arm
and dandled on her knees" (ISAIAH 66:12).

*L*et the peace of Christ
rule in your hearts . . .
you were called to peace (COLOSSIANS 3:15).

*G*race and peace to you
from God our Father
and the Lord Jesus Christ (PHILIPPIANS 1:2).

*Y*ou will keep in perfect peace
him whose mind is steadfast,
because he trusts in you (ISAIAH 26:3).

*T*he mind controlled by the Spirit
is life and peace (ROMANS 8:6).

I Am the
One Who Forgives

Troubled child,
> You feel weighted down with failure,
> as if you can't go forward.
> You *can* go forward.
> You have allowed your spiritual enemy
> to make you feel guilty for sins
> I've already forgiven.
> You have not forgiven yourself,
> so you think I have not forgiven you.

Have you forgotten my promise?
> "If we confess our sins,

he is faithful and just
and will forgive us our sins
and purify us from all
unrighteousness" (1 JOHN 1:9).
I *came* to forgive.
Everyone needs forgiveness.
Accepting my forgiveness
sets you on a new course—
a course of joy and freedom.

*B*ut when you look in the mirror,
    you see a person of failure.
    But you are not a failure.
    Circumstances do not sentence you
    to a lifetime of failure.
    You are forgiven and blessed.
    "Blessed is he whose transgressions
    are forgiven,
    whose sins are covered" (PSALM 32:1).

*E*ven though you know
    you did not commit a gross sin,
    you realize that "breaking the law"

at any point is the same as breaking it all.
That's why you need a Savior.
"He forgives all your sins" (Psalm 103:3).

*A*ll the sins of the human race
   can never exhaust my forgiveness.
   When Jesus cried out on the cross,
   "My God, my God, why have you forsaken me?"
   He was feeling the sins of the whole world.
   That's why John said,
   "Look, the Lamb of God,
   who takes away the sin of the world!" (John 1:29).

*M*y grace is sufficient for you.
   Accept my forgiveness.
   When I forgive, I choose to forget.
   Why should you keep recalling
   what I've forgotten?
   Stop living with feelings of guilt.
   I have great things in store for you.

*R*eceiving forgiveness will enable you
   to offer yourself as a channel

of my forgiving love
to flow into the lives of others.
In so doing,
you will live a life of joy and victory.

Living Words
of Scripture

*I*n him we have redemption
through his blood,
the forgiveness of sins,
in accordance with the riches
of God's grace (EPHESIANS 1:7).

*Y*ou are forgiving and good, O Lord,
abounding in love to all who call to
you (PSALM 86:5).

*Y*ou forgave the iniquity of your
people and covered all their
sins (PSALM 85:2).

*F*orgive us our sins,
    for we also forgive
    everyone who sins against us (LUKE 11:4).

*F*orgive, and you will be forgiven (LUKE 6:37).

*J*esus said, "Father, forgive them,
    for they do not know what they are
        doing" (LUKE 23:34).

*T*herefore, I tell you,
    her many sins have been forgiven—
    for she loved much.
    But he who has been forgiven little
    loves little (LUKE 7:47).

*B*e kind and compassionate to one another,
    forgiving each other,
    just as in Christ God forgave you (EPHESIANS 4:32).

*G*od made you alive with Christ.
    He forgave us all our sins,

having canceled the written code,
with its regulations,
that was against us
 and that stood opposed to us;
he took it away, nailing it to the
   cross (COLOSSIANS 2:13,14).

I will forgive their wickedness
   and will remember their sins no
      more (JEREMIAH 31:34).

11

I Am Your Shepherd

*B*eloved one,
    You expected the one who left you
    to be with you forever,
    an encourager on your path of life.
    That one failed you,
    leaving you wounded.

I am your Shepherd
    to heal your wounds,
    to comfort you,
    to care for you.

I am the *Good* Shepherd.
    I never desert those who follow me.
    I watch over you
    lovingly,
    tenderly.
    I am aware of your needs.
    You are my child.
    You shall not lack.

You have passed through troubled waters.
    I am leading you beside quiet streams.
    In quietness you will find strength
    and restoration.
    Do not hurry into new ventures.

Walk quietly with me.
    I will show you the way.
    I will guide you into paths
    that are right for you.

You need not be afraid
    of what is ahead.
    I have gone before you.

Put your hand in mine
and walk with me.

I will protect you
from all evil.
My love and my goodness
will be with you
at all times.

I am the good shepherd. . . .
I lay down my life
for my sheep (JOHN 10:14,15).

Living Words
of Scripture

*T*he LORD is my shepherd;
I shall not want. . . .
He restores my soul;
He leads me in the paths
of righteousness
for His name's sake (PSALM 23:1,3 NKJV).

*H*e tends his flock like a shepherd:
    He gathers the lambs in his arms
    and carries them close to his heart;
    he gently leads those that have
        young (ISAIAH 40:11).

*A*s a shepherd looks after
    his scattered flock
    when he is with them,
    so will I look after my sheep.
    I will rescue them
    from all the places
    where they were scattered
    on a day of clouds and darkness (EZEKIEL 34:12).

12

I Am Your Wisdom

Doubtful one,
    You need not be fearful
    regarding the path
    you are to take.
    I will provide
    reliable friends
    to counsel you.

Greater than that, *I* give you wisdom.
    Moreover, I *am* wisdom.
    Not only have I become
    your righteousness,

your holiness,
and your redemption;
I have become wisdom
within you.

Only be sensitive
to my Spirit,
to my voice,
to my indwelling presence.

Be careful never to mistake
your voice for mine,
or your desires for mine.
Listen and I will teach you.

Spend much time alone with me.
Tune out the world's clamor.
Tune into my love and wisdom.

Be among the wise who listen
and add to their learning.
Reverence of me is
the beginning of knowledge.

*I*f you listen to my wisdom
      you will dwell in safety
      and be at ease
      without fear of harm.

*T*une your ear to wisdom
      and apply your heart to understanding,
      and you will find
      the knowledge of God.

*A*lways "trust in the Lord with all your heart
      and lean not on your own understanding;
      in all your ways acknowledge him,
      and he will make your paths
         straight" (PROVERBS 3:5,6).

Living Words of Scripture

*T*he LORD gives wisdom,
      and from his mouth come knowledge
      and understanding (PROVERBS 2:6).

*W*isdom will enter your heart,
> and knowledge will be pleasant to
>> your soul (PROVERBS 2:10).

*W*isdom is supreme;
> therefore get wisdom.
> Though it cost all you have,
> get understanding (PROVERBS 4:7).

*H*e who gets wisdom loves his own soul;
> he who cherishes understanding
>> prospers (PROVERBS 19:8).

*I*t is because of him
> that you are in Christ Jesus,
> who has become for us wisdom from
>> God. . . (1 CORINTHIANS 1:30).

*H*ow much better to get wisdom than gold,
> to choose understanding rather than
>> silver! (PROVERBS 16:16).

*T*o the man who pleases him,
　　God gives wisdom, knowledge and
　　　happiness (ECCLESIASTES 2:26).

*W*isdom makes one wise man more powerful
　　than ten rulers in a city (ECCLESIASTES 7:19).

*M*y mouth will speak words of wisdom;
　　the utterance from my heart
　　will give understanding (PSALM 49:3).

*J*esus grew in wisdom and stature,
　　and in favor with God and men (LUKE 2:52).

[*T*he LORD] will be the sure foundation
　　for your times,
　　a rich store of salvation
　　and wisdom
　　and knowledge;
　　the fear of the LORD
　　is the key to this treasure (ISAIAH 33:6).

13

I Am Your Encourager

Despairing one,
　　You have felt such despair
　　you weren't sure
　　how you could go on living.
　　You cannot go on *alone*.
　　The magnitude of your problems
　　is too great
　　for you to bear alone.

But I am present
　　to encourage you.
　　You need never bear the weight alone.

Just as I was present
        with the downhearted in Bible times,
        so now I am with you
        to be your encourager.

As the psalmist David said,
        so can you say:
        "You are a shield around me,
        O LORD, my Glorious One,
        who lifts up my head" (PSALM 3:3).

Many times David was unable to feel my hand
        comforting him,
        but he knew my hand was there.
        My people are called to walk
        by faith.
        Sometimes this applies
        in the matter of
        my encouraging presence.

When you cannot *feel* my encouragement,
        know that I am there nonetheless.
        The feelings will come later.

"*T*hough the mountains be shaken
and the hills be removed,
yet my unfailing love for you
will not be shaken
nor my covenant of peace
be removed,"
says the LORD,
who has compassion on you (ISAIAH 54:10).

*T*rust me.
Doors will open for you.
I will not fail you.

Living Words of Scripture

*C*ommission Joshua, and encourage
and strengthen him (DEUTERONOMY 3:28).

*B*e strong and very courageous (Joshua 1:7).

*B*e of good courage (NUMBERS 13:20 NKJV).

*B*e strong and courageous.
>   Do not be afraid or terrified . . .
>   for the LORD your God goes with you;
>   he will never leave you nor
>   forsake you (DEUTERONOMY 31:6).

*S*ay this to Joab:
>   "Don't let this upset you. . . ."
>   Say this to encourage Joab (2 SAMUEL 11:25).

*J*esus immediately said to them:
>   "Take courage! It is I.
>   Don't be afraid" (MATTHEW 14:27).

I urge you to keep up your courage (ACTS 27:22).

*K*eep up your courage, men,
>   for I have faith in God
>   that it will happen just as he told me (ACTS 27:25).

I have told you these things,
>   so that in me you may have peace.
>   In this world you will have trouble.

But take heart!
I have overcome the world   (JOHN 16:33).

Wait on the LORD;
    be of good courage,
    and He shall strengthen your heart;
    wait, I say, on the LORD!   (PSALM 27:14 NKJV).

14

I Am Your Father

*B*eloved child,
>   I am your very own personal Father.
>   Never agree with those who say
>   I am a far-off God
>   or simply an impersonal entity
>   or a force in the universe.

I am spirit,
>   but that does not keep me
>   from being a very real Father.
>   And be assured that
>   my love for you

goes far beyond the love
any earthly father
can give his child.

My love is unconditional.
    Nothing can quench my love for you.
    I care about all
    that happens to you.
    As a loving Father,
    I am concerned
    with everything that concerns you.
    My Father-heart beats with your heart.

I will always be a father to you,
    a loving, understanding Father.
    You are my beloved daughter.
    My love for you is pure.
    My love for you is more
    than speaking words of love.
    My love is patient.
    As a patient Father,
    I never rush you.
    I know how much time
    you need for spiritual growth.

Others have been unkind to you.
> My fatherly love never can
> be rude or unkind.
> I am "a father to the fatherless,
> a defender of widows" (PSALM 68:5).
> Look to me and be at peace.

Living Words of Scripture

As the Father has loved me,
> so have I loved you (JOHN 15:9).

The Father himself loves you
> because you have loved me
> and have believed
> that I came from God (JOHN 16:27).

You did not receive
> a spirit that makes you
> a slave again to fear,
> but you received
> the Spirit of sonship.
> And by him we cry,

"Abba, Father."
The Spirit himself testifies
with our spirit
that we are God's children (Romans 8:15,16).

Anyone who has seen me
has seen the Father (JOHN 14:9).

He is the father of all who believe. . . (ROMANS 4:11).

Praise be to the God and Father
of our Lord Jesus Christ,
who has blessed us
in the heavenly realms
with every spiritual blessing in Christ (EPHESIANS 1:3).

For us there is but one God,
the Father, from whom all things came
and for whom we live;
and there is but one Lord, Jesus Christ,
through whom all things came
and through whom we live (1 CORINTHIANS 8:6).

Our fellowship is with the Father
and with his Son, Jesus Christ (1 JOHN 1:3).

15

I Am Your Counselor

*D*ear one,
>You are blessed.
>You have not accepted
>the counsel of those
>who do not walk with me.

*T*hey are like chaff
>blown by the wind
>and tossed about.
>I will deal with them
>who set themselves up

as counselors,
only to prey on innocent ones
like you.

Human counselors
are often in error.
Their counsel must be tested
by my Spirit.
But do not feel
that you have
no reliable one
to counsel you.

I am your Counselor.
I am the wonderful Counselor
of whom Isaiah prophesied:
"And he will be called
Wonderful Counselor" (ISAIAH 9:6).

I am the Counselor
who makes no error.
Tune your spiritual ears

to hear my voice.
I will counsel you
with perfect wisdom.

Look always to me
   and I will show you the way.
   I will keep you
   from going astray.
   I will teach you things
   you know not of.

I only ask that you
   dwell in my presence,
   listen to my voice,
   look at my beauty,
   taste my infinite goodness,
   follow my leading,
   enjoy my presence,
   trust me in all things.

Know that I am with you.

Living Words
of Scripture

I will praise the LORD,
who counsels me;
even at night
my heart instructs me (PSALM 16:7).

Y ou guide me with your counsel (PSALM 73:24).

H e will be called Wonderful Counselor,
Mighty God, Everlasting Father,
Prince of Peace (ISAIAH 9:6).

Y ou are great in counsel
and mighty in work,
for your eyes are open
to all the ways of the sons
of men (JEREMIAH 32:19 NKJV).

L isten to counsel
and receive instruction,
that you may be wise. . . . (PROVERBS 19:20 NKJV).

*Y*our statutes are my delight;
>they are my counselors (PSALM 119:24).

A wise man will hear
>and increase learning,
>and a man of understanding
>will attain wise counsel (PROVERBS 1:5 NKJV).

O LORD, You are my God.
>I will exalt You,
>I will praise Your name,
>for You have done wonderful things;
>Your counsels of old
>are faithfulness and truth (ISAIAH 25:1 NKJV).

*T*he counsel of the LORD
>stands forever,
>the plans of His heart
>to all generations (PSALM 33:11 NKJV).

16

I Am Your
Lily of the Valley

*F*avored one,
    You have wondered why
    you have been required
    to walk through this dark valley.
    You have felt so lonesome there.
    You have longed for the mountain heights
    where the sun shines brightly.

*Y*ou have wished for
    the sounds of other voices—
    reassuring voices

of those who would understand.
And you have found so few.

Many of my chosen ones
    must walk through similar valleys.
    Your valley is not eternal.
    It is a part of growth.
    I would like to have
    spared you the pain.

But as the cross was my preparation
    for service,
    so your valley experience
    has prepared you
    for service in my kingdom.

If you cannot grasp that just yet,
    you will later,
    and you will be glad.
    Nothing is wasted in my kingdom.
    Every experience
    surrendered to me
    is redeemed and used.

Those whose feet tread
    only on the mountaintops
    are not chosen to reap
    in the richest vineyards.
    They are not equipped
    as you are
    for my kingdom service.
    They have their reward,
    but their service
    cannot compare with yours.

You are among those whom I have singled out
    to be especially cleansed
    and sanctified for my use.
    You had to walk through the valley
    in order to know me more fully.
    I am your Comforter,
    your lily of the valley.

Living Words
of Scriptures

I am a rose of Sharon,
    a lily of the valleys (SONG OF SOLOMON 2:1).

*L*ike a lily among thorns
    is my darling among the
        maidens (SONG OF SOLOMON 2:2).

*H*e sends the springs into the valleys,
    which flow among the hills (PSALM 104:10 NKJV).

I will make rivers flow on barren heights,
    and springs within the valleys.
    I will turn the desert
    into pools of water,
    and the parched ground into springs (ISAIAH 41:18).

17

I Am Your Helper

Beloved one,
    With the one dearest to you
    no longer with you,
    you have wondered,
    Who will assist me
    with this and that?
    You have felt helpless.
    I am the helper of the helpless.

I specialize in helping those
    who are in need of my help.
    I never fail to hear the cry

of my beloved ones.
No cry is too weak to gain
my attention.

I will surely give you the help
you need.
My timing is perfect.
I never come late.
You are my care.
Your concerns are my concerns.
I am your very life,
your breath.

The enemy has come against you in might,
leaving you powerless
in your own strength.
But be not afraid.
You are not alone.
You are not on your own.
You are dear to my heart.
I am with you.

There is none like me to help the powerless
against the enemy.

91

Look to me.
Rely on me.
Depend on me.
I am your helper.
Wait in confidence for me.
Keep your spirit calm.

When the psalmist cried,
  "O Lord, be my help,"
  I heard and answered.
  I show no partiality.
  As surely as I helped him,
  I will help you.

Living Words
of Scripture

I am the Lord, your God,
  who takes hold of your right hand
  and says to you,
  "Do not fear;
  I will help you" (ISAIAH 41:13).

*Y*ou, O God,
> do see trouble and grief;
> you consider it to take it in hand (PSALM 10:14).

*S*urely God is my help;
> the Lord is the one
> who sustains me (PSALM 54:4).

*H*e will deliver the needy
> who cry out,
> the afflicted
> who have no one to help (PSALM 72:12).

*W*e say with confidence,
> "The Lord is my helper;
> I will not be afraid" (HEBREWS 13:6).

18

I Am
Your Vine

*P*recious child,
>You feel as if you have been
>separated from life,
>vulnerable
>and unattached.

*B*e assured, my beloved,
>that nothing can separate you
>from my love.
>You are a part of me.
>I am the Vine.
>You are a branch

of the Vine.
We are united.

*T*rue, you have felt the pain
of my pruning shears.
No one who grows
in spiritual maturity
can escape the pruning.
As the gardener trims
and shapes the branches
of his grapevines
to make them productive,
so must I.
But it is done in love.
Later, you will understand
and be grateful.

*Y*ou will see that it has worked
for your good,
to make you whole,
to make you complete.

*Y*ou abide vitally united to me,
your Vine.

Apart from me
you can do nothing.
Through me
you can do all things needful.
I am the strength of your life.
Cling trustfully to me,
and I will be glorified through you.

Dismiss the feeling that
you are separated from me
or from life.
Abiding in me,
you have abundant life.
You will realize
this truth as time goes on.
You are a part of life—
my life.

As life-sap flows through the branches,
so my Spirit flows through you
to sweep away your pain,
to fill you with more

of myself,
of my joy.

As the branches reach up
to receive the light of the sun,
lift up your soul
and receive the light of my love.

You are in care of the Master Gardener.
I have made you one with me.
You are rooted and grounded
in me, in my love.

Rest in that glad assurance.

*Living Words
of Scripture*

I am the true vine,
and my Father is the gardener (JOHN 15:1).

*H*e cuts off every branch in me
      that bears no fruit,
      while every branch
      that does bear fruit
      he prunes so that it will be
      even more fruitful (JOHN 15:2).

I am the vine;
      you are the branches.
      If a man remains in me
      and I in him,
      he will bear much fruit;
      apart from me you can do nothing (JOHN 15:5).

*E*very man will sit under his own vine
      and under his own fig tree,
      and no one will make them afraid,
      for the LORD Almighty has spoken (MICAH 4:4).

19

I Am Your
Rose of Sharon

Dear suffering child,
    I suffer with you in the loss
    of the endearing words you used to hear.
    I, too, longed for words I did not hear.
    You have felt the unfairness of life
    in snatching from you
    the one who called you lovely names.
    Life is unfair,
    but I am fair.
    I am never unfair.

My desire is for you to know
    that I *cannot* be unfair.
    I long for you to stay near me.
    Let my Spirit prepare your heart
    to hear me speak.
    I long for you to listen
    while I declare my love for you.

I am your Rose of Sharon,
    the lover of your soul.

Listen while I assure you
    that the wintry storm
    of your life is past.
    The boisterous winds
    and driving rains
    are over and gone.

Flowers are about to spring forth
    and appear in your life.
    You will see.
    The time of singing has come.
    In your heart you will hear
    and you will rejoice.

You will delight in me
and find joys beyond measure.
You will discover new paths
and find spiritual joy
and fulfillment
hitherto unknown to you.

You are my beloved,
and I am yours.
Come away with me
and rejoice in my all-sufficient love.
Know that in me
you live and move
and have your being.
Let every breath be a reminder
of my love for you.

Living Words
of Scripture

I am a rose of Sharon,
a lily of the valleys (SONG OF SOLOMON 2:1).

101

The LORD your God is with you,
>   he is mighty to save.
>   He will take great delight in you,
>   he will quiet you with his love,
>   he will rejoice over you with
>   singing (ZEPHANIAH 3:17).

Sing the glory of his name;
>   make his praise glorious! (PSALM 66:2).

The desert and the parched land will be glad;
>   the wilderness will rejoice and blossom.
>   Like the crocus, it will burst into bloom;
>   it will rejoice greatly and shout for joy.
>   The glory of Lebanon will be given to it,
>   the splendor of Carmel and Sharon;
>   they will see the glory of the LORD,
>   the splendor of our God (ISAIAH 35:1).

I will give you the treasures of darkness,
>   riches stored in secret places,
>   so that you may know that I am the LORD,
>   the God of Israel,
>   who summons you by name (ISAIAH 45:3).

20

I Am Your Protector

Beloved child,
    You need not feel,
    because you no longer
    have the one who was special to you,
    that you are without help.
    I am your help
    and your protector.

As I said to Abram,
    I now say to you,
    "Do not be afraid. . . .

I am your shield,
your very great reward" (GENESIS 15:1).

*R*est assured of this:
I give particular attention to those who feel
lonely,
who have no one special in their lives.
You may affirm with the psalmist:
"The Lord is my strength and my shield;
my heart trusts in him,
and I am helped" (PSALM 28:7).

I am indeed your strength,
your shield,
your protection.
I am able to protect you
from all evil,
from all harm.

I am faithful to all my promises
and loving to all my creation.
I will hide you
in the shelter of my love.

My right hand will sustain you
    and keep you from slipping into error.
    I only ask that you release all to me.
    Trust me completely.

Your loving God I will always be.
    I am your fortress
    in whom you can take refuge.
    I am always with you,
    even within you,
    to show you the way.
    I will lead you step-by-step.

Affirm with my servant Isaiah:
    "In the shadow of his hand he hid me;
    he made me into a polished arrow
    and concealed me in his quiver" (ISAIAH 49:2).

Living Words
of Scripture

Do not be afraid;
    do not be discouraged (DEUTERONOMY 1:21).

The LORD will protect him
      and preserve his life;
      he will bless him in the land
      and not surrender him
      to the desire of his foes (PSALM 41:2).

Know therefore that the LORD your God is God;
      he is the faithful God,
      keeping his covenant of love
      to a thousand generations
      of those who love him and keep his
         commands (DEUTERONOMY 7:9).

The LORD your God will bless you
      as he has promised (DEUTERONOMY 15:6).

He is the Rock,
      his works are perfect,
      and all his ways are just.
      A faithful God who does no wrong,
      upright and just is he (DEUTERONOMY 32:4).

$\mathcal{T}$he LORD loves the just
>
> and will not forsake his faithful ones.
> They will be protected forever (PSALM 37:28).

$\mathcal{Y}$ou hear, O LORD,
>
> the desire of the afflicted;
> you encourage them,
> and you listen to their cry (PSALM 10:17).

$\mathcal{I}$ trust in your unfailing love;
>
> my heart rejoices in your salvation.
> I will sing to the LORD,
> for he has been good to me (PSALM 13:5,6).

$\mathcal{Y}$our love, O LORD,
>
> reaches to the heavens,
> your faithfulness to the skies (PSALM 36:5).

21

I Am Your Defender

Beloved child,
   You have felt like a nobody
   because of the unfortunate circumstances
   which have befallen you.
   You are every bit as much
   somebody as if nothing
   ugly had happened to you.

You are not alone.
   I am present

to support you,
to defend you.
I am your defender.

I know your breaking points.
I would never put more on you
than you can bear.
Surrender your cares to me.

*A*gain, I say,
I am your defender.
I am for you.
Trust your future to me.
Keep your eyes fixed on me,
not on your circumstances.
Remember that you are mine,
and I cannot be against you.

If I am for you,
can anyone be against you?
I have conquered the world,

depriving it of its power to harm you.
I have won the victory for you.

You cannot see ahead,
  but I can.
  I hold the future.
  Your times are in my hands.
  I am in charge.
  Stand firm and you will see
  the deliverance I will bring.
  You will experience victory.

As I said to Joshua,
  so now I say to you,
  "Be strong and courageous.
  Do not be terrified;
  do not be discouraged,
  for the Lord your God
  will be with you wherever you go" (JOSHUA 1:9).

I am your maker, your defender.

Living Words
of Scripture

Let all those rejoice
        who put their trust in You;
        let them ever shout for joy,
        because You defend them;
        let those also who love Your name
        be joyful in You (PSALM 5:11 NKJV).

My defense is of God,
        who saves the upright in heart (PSALM 7:10 NKJV).

May the LORD answer you
        in the day of trouble;
        may the name of the God of Jacob
            defend you (PSALM 20:1 NKJV).

O You his Strength,
        I will wait for You,
        for God is my defense (PSALM 59:9 NKJV).

To You, O my Strength,
 I will sing praises;
 for God is my defense,
 my God of mercy (PSALM 59:17 NKJV).

He only is my rock and my salvation;
 He is my defense;
 I shall not be greatly moved (PSALM 62:2 NKJV).

Like birds flying about,
 so will the LORD of hosts defend Jerusalem.
 Defending, He will also deliver it;
 passing over, He will preserve it (ISAIAH 31:5 NKJV).

22

I Am Your Identity

*B*eloved one,
You have not lost your identity.
You identity *was* and *is*
much more than you think.
I am your identity.

*Y*ou gained your real identity
when you were merged with me—
immersed in my Spirit.
I have never looked at you and judged you
by what you have done or failed to do.

I have always said,
   "There is my beloved one—
   my child,
   one whom I purchased with my blood."
   All who turn to me
   upon being crushed
   become more aware of their real identity.
   You are among those who
   best understand what Paul meant
   when he said,
   "I have been crucified with Christ
   and I no longer live,
   but Christ lives in me" (GALATIANS 2:20).

Your identity with me—
   your relationship with me—
   is the only truly satisfying
   relationship possible.
   You are in a safe place
   when you are rightly related to me.

Your experiences have
   introduced you

to an identification
not previously known to you.

You have gone through
a type of Gethsemane.
All who choose to be
closely identified with me
sooner or later
experience their own Gethsemane.

It is always bitter,
but it serves a purpose
which later will be revealed.

Your experiences with me
will become more and more blessed.
You need never seek spiritual "highs"
in order to feel your identity with me.
Seek me for myself.
I'll take care of the rest.
You will grow in your awareness
of all that is contained
in your identification with me.

Meanwhile, rejoice in the truth
of knowing that your identity
is not lost.
Your identity is in me,
your Lord and Savior.

Living Words of Scripture

Clearly no one
is justified before God
by the law, because
"The righteous will live by faith" (GALATIANS 3:11).

The law was put in charge
to lead us to Christ
that we might be justified by faith.
Now that faith has come,
we are no longer
under the supervision
of the law (GALATIANS 3:24,25).

The only thing that counts
  is faith
  expressing itself through love (GALATIANS 5:6).

For it is by grace
  you have been saved, through faith—
  and this not from yourselves,
  it is the gift of God—
  not by works,
  so that no one can boast (EPHESIANS 2:8,9).

23

I Am Your Spiritual Husband

Beloved one,
    I am your spiritual husband.
    I know how much you sometimes long
    for a human touch when there is none.
    I, too, sometimes felt
    that yearning
    before I endured the cross.

I felt what you feel.
    Therefore I am able to satisfy
    in a supernatural way

that longing in your soul.
I satisfy in a way
the world cannot understand.
I am a devoted husband.

Stretch forth your hands to me.
    Lift up your heart to my throne.
    I will take away your loneliness
    and comfort you
    as only I can do.
    I am a faithful husband.

Truly, your desire is toward me.
    I will reward your faithfulness.
    You will not be disappointed.
    I will never desert you.
    I am a trustworthy husband.

You have sought my will and
    placed your trust in me.
    I never forsake those who seek me.
    I am a patient husband.

*W*eeping may remain for a night.
      The night may seem long.
      But rejoicing comes in the morning.
      I am your joy-bringing husband.

" *D*o not be afraid;
      you will not suffer shame. . . .
      For your Maker is your husband—
      the LORD Almighty is his name—
      the Holy One of Israel
      is your Redeemer" (ISAIAH 54:4,5).

*M*y love for you
      is far greater
      than any earthly husband
      could ever give you.

*A*ccept my love and be blessed.

Living Words
of Scripture

" *T*hough the mountains be shaken
      and the hills be removed,

yet my unfailing love for you
will not be shaken
nor my covenant of peace be removed,"
says the LORD,
who has compassion on you (ISAIAH 54:10).

I am jealous for you
with a godly jealousy.
I promised you to one husband,
to Christ,
so that I might present you
as a pure virgin to him (2 CORINTHIANS 11:2).

In Christ
all the fullness of the Deity
lives in bodily form,
and you have been given fullness
in Christ,
who is the head over every power
and authority (COLOSSIANS 2:9,10).

24

I Am
Your Joy

𝓑eloved one,
    You have felt many times
    as if you might never again
    know joy and gladness.
    I say unto you,
    before long
    your heart will sing for joy.
    I live within you
    to be your joy.

𝒴our sorrow will pass.
    You will look back at this period

of your life
and say,
"It was like a mist
that appeared for a time
and then vanished."

While you're walking in sorrow
time seems like eternity.
But after you have passed through,
you will say,
"My Lord was there all the time.
His joy sustained me."

I came not only
to comfort all who mourn
but "to bestow on them
a crown of beauty
instead of ashes,
the oil of gladness
instead of mourning,
and a garment of praise
instead of a spirit of despair" (ISAIAH 61:3).

I am crowning you with a crown of beauty,
the beauty of joy.

I am anointing you
with the oil of gladness.

In your joy,
you will put on a garment of praise.
Joy will be the ruler
of your inner dwelling.
Soon your joy will spill over
into the hearts of others.
And they will join you
in singing for joy.

Living Words
of Scripture

You have made known to me the path of life;
you will fill me with joy in your presence,
with eternal pleasures at your right
hand (PSALM 16:11).

Weeping may remain for a night,
but rejoicing comes in the morning (PSALM 30:5).

124

I go to the altar of God,
>   to God, my joy and my delight.
>   I will praise you with the harp, O God, my
>   God.
>   Why are you downcast, O my soul?
>   Why so disturbed within me?
>   Put your hope in God,
>   for I will yet praise him,
>   my Savior and my God (Psalm 43:4,5).

He brought out his people with rejoicing,
>   his chosen ones with shouts of joy (PSALM 105:43).

I will rejoice over [you]
>   and take delight in [you] (ISAIAH 65:19).

God gives wisdom and knowledge
>   and joy to a man who is good in
>   His sight (ECCLESIASTES 2:26 NKJV).

You have enlarged the nation
>   and increased their joy;

they rejoice before you
as people rejoice at the harvest (ISAIAH 9:3).

Once more the humble will rejoice in the LORD;
the needy will rejoice in the Holy One of
Israel (ISAIAH 29:19).

The ransomed of the LORD will return.
They will enter Zion with singing;
everlasting joy will crown their heads.
Gladness and joy will overtake them,
and sorrow and sighing will flee
away (ISAIAH 35:10).

Burst into songs of joy together . . .
for the LORD has comforted his
people (ISAIAH 52:9).

25

I Am Your Righteousness

*D*ear confused child,
>   You are fretting about your past,
>   feeling guilty about the sins
>   you have already confessed to me.

*A*re you forgetting who I am?
>   I am the one who forgives
>   all your iniquities.

I have buried all
>   your sins in the deepest sea.
>   There they must stay.

You have been cleansed
by the blood of the Lamb.

Rest in the knowledge
that when you repent
I remember your sins no more.

They are covered
by the blood of my Son,
who gave His life for you.
You are free to live joyfully in Him
now and forever.

Your righteousness is dependent
not upon anything you do
or fail to do,
but upon your faith in me.

It is by grace
and grace alone
that you are saved
and kept secure in me.

You did nothing to earn
　　your salvation.
　　You simply repented
　　of your sin
　　and allowed me
　　to come into your heart.

You trusted in the power of the blood
　　of the cross to save you,
　　and now you are living
　　in fellowship with me.
　　That is all you need to do
　　in order to be declared righteous.

The apostle Paul knew
　　that his righteousness
　　came not from anything he
　　did, or failed to do,
　　but from his faith in me.
　　He said, "not having a righteousness
　　of my own that comes from the law,
　　but that which is through faith in Christ

129

—the righteousness that comes from God
and is by faith" (PHILIPPIANS 3:9).
You can make the same declaration.
You are righteous through me.

*Y*ou are not to give in to
    religiosity
    or legalism.
    You are mine.
    I am not only
    your forgiver but also
    your Redeemer.

*A*s your Redeemer,
    I am ready to restore
    all that the power of sin
    has taken from you.

*B*ecause of the righteousness of Israel,
    Isaiah predicted
    that no weapon
    formed against them
    would prevail (SEE ISAIAH 54:17).

The same is true
for my children today.

Since your forgiveness is based
not on what you do,
but on what my Son did
at Calvary,
can you not live in that blessedness?

As a righteous person
you "may have many troubles,
but the LORD delivers [you]
from them all" (PSALM 34:19).

When troubles come your way
you are not to think
that I have forgotten you.
I can never forget you.
I will deliver you in due time.
Wait on me.
Trust me.

Salvation cost the life of my Son,
but it's free to you.

131

Rejoice in it.
Rejoice in *me.*
Rejoice in life itself.

I am righteous in all my ways.
Look to me.
Trust in me.
Rely on me.
Find your joy in me.
I am yours; you are mine.

"*M*ay the righteous be glad
and rejoice before God;
may they be happy
and joyful" (PSALM 68:3).

*Th*is, dear child, is my desire for you.

Living Words
of Scripture

*A*nd I—in righteousness
I will see your face;

when I awake,
I will be satisfied
with seeing your likeness (PSALM 17:15).

*A*nswer me when I call to you,
O my righteous God.
Give me relief from my distress;
be merciful to me and hear my prayer (PSALM 4:1).

I will betroth you to me forever;
I will betroth you in righteousness
and justice,
in love
and compassion (HOSEA 2:19).

*M*y righteousness draws near speedily,
my salvation is on the way (ISAIAH 51:5).

*M*y righteousness will last forever,
my salvation through all generations (ISAIAH 51:8).

*T*he LORD has made his salvation known
and revealed his righteousness to the
nations (PSALM 98:2).

133

It is because of him
    that you are in Christ Jesus,
    who has become for us wisdom from God—
    that is, our righteousness,
    holiness and redemption (1 CORINTHIANS 1:30).

God made him who had no sin
    to be sin for us,
    so that in him
    we might become
    the righteousness of God (2 CORINTHIANS 5:21).

Christ died for sins
    once for all,
    the righteous for the unrighteous,
    to bring you to God (1 PETER 3:18).

[Righteousness, standing acceptable to God]
    will be granted and accredited
    to us also who believe in
    (trust in, adhere to, and rely on) God,
    who raised Jesus our Lord from the
        dead (ROMANS 4:24 AMP).

Christ is the end of the law
  so that there may be righteousness
  for everyone who believes (ROMANS 10:4).

If, by the trespass of the one man,
  death reigned through that one man,
  how much more will those
  who receive God's abundant provision
  of grace
  and of the gift of righteousness
  reign in life
  through the one man, Jesus Christ (ROMANS 5:17).

Through the obedience of the one man
  the many will be made righteous (ROMANS 5:19).

Put on the new self,
  created to be like God
  in true righteousness
  and holiness (EPHESIANS 4:24).

26

I Am
Your Life

*D*ear one,
   You have allowed your circumstances
   to cause you to despair of life.
   Remember, I am your life.

*R*efuse to side with negative forces
   that would suggest that you can create
   life within yourself.
   Only *I* am capable of that.
   But I create life *within* you.

"I have come that [you] may have life,
        and have it to the full" (JOHN 10:10).
        This is as true for you
        as it was to those
        to whom it was first spoken.

To have a full life does not mean
        you are free from trials.
        But it includes the fact that
        I am with you in every trial
        for your blessing.

Through your trials,
        I take you from faith
        to faith,
        from strength
        to strength.
        Dare to believe it.

You may feel as if you're
        walking through a dark valley
        or about to step off a precipice.

*B*ut I, the Lord of life,
>   am holding your hand.
>   I will show you the path of life.   (SEE PSALM 16:11.)

I have you told you
>   you are righteous through me.

I am the Bread of Life.
>   I am the way,
>   the truth,
>   and the life.

*D*eclare with the apostle Paul:
>   "I have been crucified with Christ
>   and I no longer live,
>   but Christ lives in me.
>   The life I live in the body,
>   I live by faith in the Son of God,
>   who loved me
>   and gave himself for me"   (GALATIANS 2:20).

*Y*ou see,
>   whoever has *me* has life.
>   *I* am your life.

I am the only life there is.
I express life through you
as you yield to me
as your true life.

Living Words
of Scripture

I have set before you life. . . .
Now choose life (DEUTERONOMY 30:19).

*T*his is what the LORD says:
"See, I am setting before you
the way of life . . ." (JEREMIAH 21:8).

*I*n the way of righteousness
there is life;
along that path is immortality (PROVERBS 12:28).

*T*he fear of the LORD
is a fountain of life,
turning a man
from the snares of death (PROVERBS 14:27).

*I*n him [Jesus] was life,
and that life was the light of men (JOHN 1:4).

*J*esus declared,
"I am the bread of life" (JOHN 6:35).

*T*he Spirit gives life . . . .
The words I have spoken to you
are spirit and they are life (JOHN 6:63).

I am the light of the world.
Whoever follows me
will never walk in darkness,
but will have the light of life (JOHN 8:12).

I am the resurrection
and the life.
He who believes in me will live,
even though he dies (JOHN 11:25).

*T*hese are written
that you may believe
that Jesus is the Christ,
the Son of God,

and that by believing
you may have life in his name (JOHN 20:31).

If Christ is in you,
your body is dead because of sin,
yet your spirit is alive
because of righteousness (ROMANS 8:10).

The Spirit gives life (2 CORINTHIANS 3:6).

For you died,
and your life is now hidden
with Christ in God (COLOSSIANS 3:3).

. . . according to the promise
of life that is in Christ Jesus (2 TIMOTHY 1:1).

He who has the Son has life (1 JOHN 5:12).

With you is the fountain of life;
in your light we see light (PSALM 36:9).

The truly righteous man
attains life (PROVERBS 11:19).

27

I Am
Your Shield

Dear waiting child,
You have waited long
for the fulfillment of your desires.
You are near the point of despair,
tired of waiting,
afraid to trust,
doubtful if your dreams
will ever come true,
wondering if your dreams
have been in vain.

But I say to you,
"Wait for the LORD;

be strong and take heart
and wait for the LORD" (PSALM 27:14).
I am your Lord.
I am your shield.
Trust me to work
in your behalf.

My timing is always perfect.
I am always on time.
Recapture your dreams.
Wait patiently.
I will not be late.

Declare with the psalmist,
"I wait for the LORD,
my soul waits,
and in his word
I put my hope" (PSALM 130:5).

Put your hope
and trust in me.
Wait in confidence.
I will not fail you.
Be not afraid.

I am your help and your shield.

143

Living Words
of Scripture

I am your shield,
> your very great reward (GENESIS 15:1).

*H*e is your shield
> and helper
> and your glorious sword (DEUTERONOMY 33:29).

*W*e wait in hope for the LORD;
> he is our help and our shield (PSALM 33:20).

*Y*ou are a shield around me, O LORD;
> you bestow glory on me and lift up
>> my head (PSALM 3:3).

*S*urely, O LORD,
> you bless the righteous;
> you surround them with your favor
> as with a shield (PSALM 5:12).

You give me your shield of victory,
and your right hand sustains me;
you stoop down to make me great (PSALM 18:35).

The LORD is my strength and my shield;
my heart trusts in him,
and I am helped.
My heart leaps for joy
and I will give thanks to him in song (PSALM 28:7).

He will cover you with his feathers,
and under his wings you will find refuge;
his faithfulness will be your shield and
rampart (PSALM 91:4).

You who fear him, trust in the LORD—
he is their help and shield (PSALM 115:11).

For the LORD God is a sun and shield;
the LORD bestows favor and honor;
no good thing does he withhold
from those whose walk is blameless (PSALM 84:11).

I Am Your
Intercessor

*D*ear forlorn child,
    You are feeling deserted,
    but you are not alone.
    You feel as if no one cares,
    that no one is praying for you
    during this time of your need.

*Y*ou would like to call someone
    to intercede for you,
    but you fear being misunderstood.
    I am your intercessor
    who loves and understands.

Just as I prayed for the disciples
when I lived in my fleshly body,
I pray for you now.

"My prayer is not for them alone.
I pray also for those
who will believe in me
through their message" (JOHN 17:20).
You can see from those words
that I prayed for you
even before you were born.
You were included in my prayer
to the Father as I talked to him
about my disciples.

I prayed constantly on earth;
I still pray constantly,
making intercession for you.
It doesn't matter
how many accusations
your spiritual enemy
may bring against you.
I am your advocate.
I am for you.

147

"*B*ut if anybody does sin,
    we have one who speaks to the Father
    in our defense—
    Jesus Christ, the Righteous One" (1 JOHN 2:1).

Living Words
of Scripture

*W*e do not know what we ought to pray for,
    but the Spirit himself
    intercedes for us
    with groans that words cannot express.
    And he who searches our hearts
    knows the mind of the Spirit,
    because the Spirit
    intercedes for the saints
    in accordance with God's will (ROMANS 8:26,27).

*C*hrist Jesus, who died—
    more than that,
    who was raised to life—
    is at the right hand of God
    and is also interceding for us (ROMANS 8:34).

*H*e always lives
>   to intercede for [us] (HEBREWS 7:25).

*H*e bore the sin of many,
>   and made intercession for the
>   transgressors (ISAIAH 53:12).

*H*e is able to save completely
>   those who come to God through him,
>   because he always lives
>   to intercede for them (HEBREWS 7:25).

29

I Am Your
High Priest

Dear confused child,
    You have felt
    that you had no high priest,
    no one of authority
    to properly instruct you.
    no one to stand for you.

I am your High Priest.
    As Aaron was a high priest,
    a symbol of Christ in the Old Testament,
    appointed to bless the children of Israel,

I am your High Priest.
More surely than Aaron blessed
the children of Israel,
I delight to bless you.
I speak with greater authority
than Aaron was able to do.

I am in glory right now,
    arrayed in high-priestly garments.
    I stand before the Father in your behalf.

For Christ did not enter a man-made sanctuary
    that was only a copy of the true one;
    he entered heaven itself,
    now to appear for us
    in God's presence (HEBREWS 9:24).

The devil, your accuser,
    stood before the throne
    to question Job's righteousness.
    He stands before God right now to accuse you,
    but you need not fear.
    I stand between him and

151

his accusations against you.
You are mine to defend and protect.
I take care of you.

I take no pleasure in having to discipline you.
I do take pleasure in blessing you.
As Jesus said to His disciples,
I say to you,
"Do not be afraid . . .
for your Father has been pleased
to give you the kingdom" (LUKE 12:32).

I understand all your problems and temptations.
In my flesh I suffered temptations
of all kinds.
It doesn't matter what you're feeling
or what you've been through,
I have felt it.
I understand all you're going through.

As the Scripture says:
"For this reason
he had to be made

like his brothers in every way,
in order that he might become
a merciful and faithful high priest
in service to God,
and that he might make atonement
for the sins of the people.

*B*ecause he himself suffered
when he was tempted,
he is able to help those
who are being tempted" (HEBREWS 2:17,18).

*N*othing you experience escapes my notice.
I am your High Priest
who cares for you at all times
and in every situation.

Living Words of Scripture

[*J*esus] was designated by God
to be high priest
in the order of Melchizedek (HEBREWS 5:10).

153

The LORD has sworn
> and will not change his mind:
> "You [the Lord] are a priest forever,
> in the order of Melchizedek." (PSALM 110:4).

Therefore, holy brothers,
> who share in the heavenly calling,
> fix your thoughts on Jesus,
> the apostle and high priest whom we
> > confess (HEBREWS 3:1).

We do have such a high priest,
> who sat down at the right hand
> of the throne of the Majesty in heaven,
> and who serves in the sanctuary,
> the true tabernacle set up
> by the Lord, not by man (HEBREWS 8:1,2).

Therefore, since we have a great high priest
> who has gone through the heavens,
> Jesus the Son of God,
> let us hold firmly to the faith we
> > profess (HEBREWS 4:14).

*W*e do not have a high priest
    who is unable to sympathize
    with our weaknesses,
    but we have one who
    has been tempted in every way,
    just as we are—yet was without sin (HEBREWS 4:15).

*S*uch a high priest meets our need—
    one who is holy, blameless, pure,
    set apart from sinners,
    exalted above the heavens (HEBREWS 7:26).

*W*hen Christ came as high priest
    of the good things that are already here,
    he went through the greater
    and more perfect tabernacle
    that is not man-made,
    that is to say,
    not a part of this creation.
    He did not enter by means
    of the blood of goats and calves;
    but he entered the Most Holy Place
    once for all by his own blood,

155

having obtained eternal
redemption (HEBREWS 9:11,12).

Therefore, brothers
since we have confidence
to enter the Most Holy Place
by the blood of Jesus,
by a new and living way
opened for us through the curtain,
that is, his body,
and since we have a great priest
over the house of God,
let us draw near to God
with a sincere heart
in full assurance of faith,
having our hearts sprinkled
to cleanse us from a guilty conscience
and having our bodies washed with
pure water (HEBREWS 10:19-22).

30

I Am
Your Refuge

Discouraged child,
    You have felt vulnerable and afraid,
    as if there were no place of refuge,
    no place of safety for you.

In the time of Moses
    I established cities of refuge
    for those who were pursued.
    They could dwell there
    until the time of safety.

I am here to remind you that
    I am your refuge.

You can take refuge in me at any time.
I am always available
to you and for you.

As the psalmist prayed, so can you:
"In you, O LORD, I have taken refuge;
let me never be put to shame.
Rescue me and deliver me in your
    righteousness;
turn your ear to me and save me.
Be my rock of refuge,
to which I can always go;
give the command to save me,
for you are my rock and my
    fortress" (PSALM 71:1-3).

I heard and answered David's prayer.
Just as surely as I heard his prayer,
I will hear yours.
You are as valuable to me as David was.
David knew I was his refuge
in his times of trouble.
You too can be assured
of my presence with you.

158

At a later time
David declared,
"Praise be to the LORD my Rock,
who trains my hands for war,
my fingers for battle.
He is my loving God
and my fortress,
my stronghold
and my deliverer,
my shield, in whom I take refuge" (PSALM 144:1,2).

I am the same God now as I was then.
Be assured that you can take refuge in me.
Indeed, I am your refuge.

Living Words
of Scripture

The eternal God is your refuge,
and underneath are the everlasting
arms (DEUTERONOMY 33:27).

159

Let the righteous rejoice in the LORD
    and take refuge in him;
    let all the upright in heart praise
        him! (PSALM 64:10).

The salvation
    of the [consistently] righteous
    is of the LORD;
    He is their Refuge
    and secure Stronghold
    in the time of trouble (PSALM 37:39 AMP).

I have become like a portent to many,
    but you are my strong refuge (PSALM 71:7).

God is our refuge and strength,
    an ever-present help in trouble (PSALM 46:1).

The LORD of hosts is with us;
    the God of Jacob is our refuge (PSALM 46:7 NKJV).

My salvation
and my honor
depend on God;
he is my mighty rock,
my refuge (PSALM 62:7).

I Am Your God Most High

*D*ear child,
  You have felt like
  an insignificant person.
  Without my presence,
  you would be.
  But I am the God Most High.
  I am *your* God.

I always have the last word
  in every situation.
  And my word is victorious.

Because you dwell in me and I in you,
    victory can be yours.

Remember, you are seated with me
    in heavenly places,
    far above any problem
    which may come against you.

Meditate on this truth
    until it grips you,
    until you feel differently
    about your situation.

As God Most High, I am your blesser.
    That is one of my characteristics.
    My desire and purpose
    is to bless my people.

As a believer, you are one of my people.
    Therefore, you are blessed.
    Become aware of your blessings
    under my authority as your
    Most High God,

the God of all power
and authority.

Your spiritual enemy may come against
you with feelings
of despair,
depression,
and defeat.

The enemy may throw fiery darts at you,
but the victory is yours through
your God Most High.
Receive it in Jesus' name.

Walk in the authority which is yours
through your Savior, Jesus Christ.
Only let your life reflect
your position in Christ.

You are His, a child of the Most High God.

Living Words
of Scripture

Blessed be Abram by God Most High,
  Creator of heaven and earth.
  And blessed be God Most High (GENESIS 14:19,20).

My own hand laid
    the foundations of the earth,
    and my right hand
    spread out the heavens;
    when I summon them,
    they all stand up together (ISAIAH 48:13).

All authority in heaven
    and on earth has been given
      to me (MATTHEW 28:18).

I will give thanks to the LORD
    because of his righteousness

and will sing praise to the name
of the LORD Most High (PSALM 7:17).

I will be glad and rejoice in you;
I will sing praise to your name,
O Most High (PSALM 9:2).

It is my pleasure to tell you
about the miraculous signs and wonders
that the Most High God has performed
for me (DANIEL 4:2).

The Most High is sovereign
over the kingdoms of men. . . (DANIEL 4:17).

The Most High does not live
in houses made by men.
As the prophet says:
"Heaven is my throne,
and the earth is my footstool. . . " (ACTS 7:48,49).

*Y*our righteousness reaches to the skies,
  O God, you who have done great things.
  Who, O God, is like you? (PSALM 71:19).

*Y*ou, O LORD, are the Most High
  over all the earth;
  you are exalted far above all gods (PSALM 97:9).

32

I Am the Creative God

*D*ear faltering child,
> You need not feel guilty
> for your frailties and
> your tendencies to weakness.
> Neither need you feel like a failure
> when you are unable to accomplish
> all you would like to.
> Only *I* am to do that.

I am the great Creator.
> Creator is one of my names.

One of the Hebrew words
for my name is *Elohim*.
It means I am the true God.
Sometimes it is plural,
as "In the beginning God . . . " (GENESIS 1:1).

Elohim means I am the God
        of trinity—
        God the Father, God the Son,
        and God the Holy Spirit.

The word also implies
        that I am a God of several powers,
        many resources, many majesties,
        much glory, and absolute authority.
        By the power of my word
        I formed the worlds.
        I brought order out of chaos.
        I still do.

I am omnipotent, the God of all power.
        Because of my great love,
        I use my power in behalf of my children.

As Creator, I am a covenant-keeping God.
As surely as I made a covenant
with Abraham, I have a covenant with you.
When I make a promise,
you can be sure of its fulfillment.
I never break a promise.

There is blessing and comfort
in knowing my name as *Elohim*.
My name signifies
supreme power,
sovereignty,
and glory.

Rest in the assurance that
I, your great Creator,
am always with you
and for you.

Since I am Creator
and you are created in my image,
you too are able to create.
What would you like to do?

What dreams do you have buried within?
Uncover the dreams that are planted in your
    heart.
Be fulfilled in me by carrying out those dreams.

Nothing is impossible with *Elohim.*

Living Words of Scripture

The LORD your God is God
    of gods and Lord of lords,
    the great God,
    mighty and awesome,
    who shows no partiality (DEUTERONOMY 10:17).

I will be the God
    of all the clans of Israel,
    and they will be my people (JEREMIAH 31:1).

I will make
    an everlasting covenant with them:

171

I will never stop doing good to
them   (JEREMIAH 32:40).

I have made you known to them,
and will continue
to make you known
in order that
the love you have for me
may be in them and
that I myself may be in them   (JOHN 17:26).

*D*o you not know?
Have you not heard?
The LORD is the everlasting God,
the Creator of the ends of the earth   (ISAIAH 40:28).

I am the LORD, your Holy One,
Israel's Creator, your King   (ISAIAH 43:15).

*L*et them praise the name of the LORD,
for he commanded and they were
created   (PSALM 148:5).

*L*ift your eyes and look to the heavens:
>   Who created all these?
>   He who brings out the starry host one by one,
>   and calls them each by name (ISAIAH 40:26).

*B*y him all things were created:
>   things in heaven and on earth,
>   visible and invisible,
>   whether thrones or powers
>   or rulers or authorities;
>   all things were created by him and
>   for him (COLOSSIANS 1:16).

33

I Am Your
God Almighty

Dear weak child,
> You have felt helplessly weak,
> as if you had no strength to accomplish
> anything you desire.
> You have thought you might as well give up
> and not try anymore.
> It is when you are weak
> that you are strong in me.

To experience my sufficiency,
> you must realize
> your own insufficiency.

I am your God Almighty.
  The Hebrew word is *El-Shaddai*.
  The word means
  the ever-existent One,
  the eternal,
  The One continually revealing
  Himself,
  His ways,
  His purposes.

*N*othing is impossible
  with *El-Shaddai*.

*N*othing is too hard for me.
  When you need me, I am present
  to help you,
  to sustain you,
  to nourish you.

*T*he psalmist knew me as his *El-Shaddai*.
  He said:
  "It is God who arms me
  with strength
  and makes my way perfect" (PSALM 18:32).

What I did for the psalmist
I am able to do for you.
I am the all-sufficient God,
the all-bountiful God.
I abundantly bless my children.
My resources are inexhaustible.

Thinking of my bounty, Isaiah wrote:
"Rejoice with Jerusalem
and be glad for her,
all you who love her;
rejoice greatly with her,
all you who mourn over her.
For you will nurse
and be satisfied . . . .
You will drink deeply
and delight
in her overflowing abundance" (ISAIAH 66:10,11).

I am sufficient for all things.
I am able to carry out my plans
to the fullest.
I am not only able

but willing—
willing to be
all you need me to be for you.

Paul said it like this:
"Now to him
who is able
to do immeasurably more
than all we ask or imagine . . .
to him be glory
in the church
and in Christ Jesus
throughout all generations,
for ever and ever! Amen" (EPHESIANS 3:20).

I am the giver of
"every good and perfect gift" (JAMES 1:17).

I never weary of pouring out my mercies
and blessings upon my people.
Only remember that my strength
is made perfect in your weakness.

Living Words
of Scripture

When Abram was ninety-nine years old,
   the LORD appeared to him and said,
   "I am God Almighty;
   walk before me and be blameless" (GENESIS 17:1).

May God Almighty bless you
   and make you fruitful
   and increase your numbers
   until you become a community of
      peoples (GENESIS 28:3).

He who dwells in the shelter
   of the Most High will rest
   in the shadow of the Almighty (PSALM 91:1).

Holy, holy, holy is the Lord God Almighty,
   who was, and is, and is to come (REVELATION 4:8).

Yes, Lord God Almighty,
   true and just are your
   judgments (REVELATION 16:7).

34

I Am Your
Lord and Master

Child of mine,
    You were told that
    you should be master of your life.
    You were misinformed.
    It is true that I gave you a free will.
    I do not wish to manipulate you,
    but I do want to guide you.
    I am your Lord and Master.
    Discipline yourself, yes.
    But you are not the controller
    of your life.
    I will guide you if you allow me to.

"For you have only one Master" (MATTHEW 23:8).
"You call me Teacher and Lord,
and you say well, for so I am" (JOHN 13:13 NKJV).

*A*s your Master, I am your help
and protection.
The word *Master* comes from
the Hebrew word *Adonai.*
It claims a right
to your obedience
and service.

*L*ord is a related word.
If I am your Lord,
I have a claim on your life.
If you try to be Lord of your own life,
you will make mistakes which you will regret.

*W*hen I require a task of you,
I will equip you for that service.
"Know that the LORD
has set apart
the godly for himself" (PSALM 4:3).

I work only for your good.
"Blessed is the [person]
whose God is the LORD,
the people he chose
for his inheritance" (PSALM 33:12).

You are not your own.
You have been bought with a price,
the blood of Jesus Himself.
Honor Him in all your decisions,
and you will be blessed.

Living Words of Scripture

Know that the LORD is God;
besides him there is no other (DEUTERONOMY 4:35).

Ascribe to the LORD
the glory due his name (1 CHRONICLES 16:29).

O LORD, our Lord,
how majestic is your name
in all the earth! (PSALM 8:1).

The eyes of the LORD
>are on those who fear him,
>on those whose hope
>is in his unfailing love (PSALM 33:18).

The LORD is gracious and righteous;
>our God is full of compassion (PSALM 116:5).

You call me "Teacher" and "Lord,"
>and rightly so, for that is what I am (JOHN 13:13).

He who is both their Master
>and yours is in heaven,
>and there is no favoritism with
>>him (EPHESIANS 6:9).

A student is not above his teacher,
>nor a servant above his master (MATTHEW 10:24).

No one can serve two masters.
>Either he will hate the
>one and love the other,
>or he will be devoted to the one
>and despise the other (MATTHEW 6:24).

35

I Am Your Sanctifier

*D*ear one,
    You have felt
    as if your life had no purpose.
    You are mistaken.

*Y*our life has purpose
    simply because you are mine.
    As surely as I said to Jeremiah,
    I say also to you,
    "Before I formed you in the womb
    I knew you;

before you were born
I sanctified you" (JEREMIAH 1:5 NKJV).

*S*anctify is one
   of the most important words
   in the Bible.
   It means to set apart,
   to separate,
   to dedicate,
   to make holy.

I am your sanctifier,
   the One who makes you holy.
   "He who sanctifies
   and those who are being sanctified
   are all of one,
   for which reason
   He is not ashamed
   to call them brethren" (HEBREWS 2:11 NKJV).

I made you holy, sanctified you,
   by giving my Son for you
   and making you my own.

"We have been sanctified
through the offering
of the body of Jesus Christ
once for all" (HEBREWS 10:10 NKJV).

I, your holy God, desire holy people.
I want to impart to you
the beauty of my holiness.

In the Old Testament,
I chose to separate my people
from the people around them
in order to keep them from
the corrupt practices of their day.
I want you to be separated
from the world's unholy practices.

As I told Moses to inform the people,
so also I say to you,
"Be holy because I,
the LORD your God, am holy" (LEVITICUS 19:2).

A holy God requires holy people.
The psalmist David said,

"One thing I ask of the LORD,
this is what I seek:
that I may dwell in the house
of the LORD all the days of my life,
to gaze upon the beauty of the LORD
and to seek him in his temple" (PSALM 27:4).

To see "the beauty of the Lord"
is to see my holiness.
It is my desire
to impart my beauty
and my holiness to you.

In another place the psalmist said,
"Let the beauty of the LORD
our God be upon us" (PSALM 90:17 NKJV).

My people of the Old Testament
knew me as Jehovah, a holy God,
who was their sanctifier.
What I, Jehovah, was

to the people of that time
the Lord Jesus Christ is to you today.

As my sanctified child,
you participate in my nature.
My holiness is imparted to you.
I only ask that you walk in holiness.

What Paul wrote to my people of Rome
applies to you:

Therefore I urge you . . .
in view of God's mercy,
to offer your bodies
as living sacrifices,
holy and pleasing to God—
this is your spiritual act of worship (ROMANS 12:1).

And Peter said,
"Just as he who called you is holy,
so be holy in all you do;
for it is written:
'Be holy, because I am holy'" (1 PETER 1:15,16).

Living Words
of Scripture

Consecrate yourselves
   and be holy,
   because I am the LORD your God.
   Keep my decrees and follow them.
   I am the LORD, who makes you
      holy (LEVITICUS 20:7,8).

God's temple is sacred,
   and you are that temple (1 CORINTHIANS 3:17).

You were washed,
   you were sanctified,
   you were justified
   in the name of the Lord Jesus Christ
   and by the Spirit of our God (1 CORINTHIANS 6:11).

May God himself,
   the God of peace,
   sanctify you through and through.

May your whole spirit,
>   soul and body
>   be kept blameless. . . (1 THESSALONIANS 5:23).

Just as he who called you is holy,
>   so be holy in all you do;
>   for it is written:
>   "Be holy, because I am holy" (1 PETER 1:15,16).

You are a chosen people,
>   a royal priesthood,
>   a holy nation,
>   a people belonging to God,
>   that you may declare the praises
>   of him who called you
>   out of darkness
>   into his wonderful light (1 PETER 2:9).

He chose us in him
>   before the creation of the world
>   to be holy
>   and blameless in his sight (EPHESIANS 1:4).

36

I Am
Your Hope

Dear discouraged one,
  You have felt hopeless
  because of the things
  that have happened to you.
  You wonder if there is any reason
  to hope any more.

Outside of me and my love,
  no one has reason to hope.
  Life's offerings are futile.
  But in me there is abundant hope.

In the Old Testament Habakkuk despaired
    because of the condition of Israel.
    I reminded him that the righteous
    will be cared for in the time of trouble.

In the end, Habakkuk's faith soared above doubt
    and feelings of hopelessness.
    He declared,
    "Though the fig tree does not bud
    and there are no grapes on the vines,
    though the olive crop fails
    and the fields produce no food,
    though there are no sheep in the pens
    and no cattle in the stalls,
    yet I will rejoice in the LORD,
    I will be joyful in God my
        Savior" (HABAKKUK 3:17,18).

As Habakkuk kept his faith strong
    by looking beyond circumstances,
    so can you.
    I see your plight,
    and I want to renew your hope.

I want to remind you that I am your hope.
You can declare with the psalmist,
"But now, Lord, what do I look for?
My hope is in you" (PSALM 39:7).

*R*ecall the times I have been with you in the past
and remember that I have not changed.
Your spiritual adversary of this world
wants to destroy your hope.
But "the one who is in you
is greater than the one
who is in the world" (1 JOHN 4:4).

*Y*ou may regard hope as a finger pointing
to a closed door.
Any time a door is closed
to one of my children,
another and better one will open.
You have only to look for it
and wait in expectation.
Take a positive look at your closed doors.
Envision another door
being opened for you.

You may sing to me,
"Praise be to the LORD your God,
who has delighted in you" (1 KINGS 10:9).

When you realize how much I delight in you,
you will begin to delight in me.
That will bring delight to my heart.
Immerse yourself in the thought
that I really do delight in you.

Living Words
of Scripture

He delivered me
because He delighted in me (2 SAMUEL 22:20 AMP).

The prayer of the upright
is His delight! (PROVERBS 15:8 AMP).

Delight yourself in the LORD
and he will give you the desires
of your heart (PSALM 37:4).

"*I* delight to do Your will, O my God,
and Your law is within my
heart (PSALM 40:8 NKJV).

In the multitude of my anxieties within me,
Your comforts delight my soul (PSALM 94:19 NKJV).

Trouble and distress have come upon me,
but your commands are my
delight (PSALM 119:143).

Then you shall delight yourself in the LORD;
and I will cause you to ride
on the high hills of the earth (ISAIAH 58:14 NKJV).

[*Not* in your own strength]
for it is God who is all the while
effectually at work in you
[energizing and creating in you
the power and desire],
both to will and to work

for His good pleasure
and satisfaction
and delight (PHILIPPIANS 2:13 AMP).

Rejoice in the Lord always
[delight, gladden yourselves in Him];
again I say, Rejoice! (PHILIPPIANS 4:4 AMP).

40

I Am Your Rock

$\mathcal{D}$ear unstable child,
    You feel as unstable
    as the foolish man
    who built his house on shifting sand.
    When the storms came, his house crashed.
    You have allowed the storms of your life
    to make you feel as if your house
    of life has crashed.
    It hasn't.
    You only feel that way.

You have forgotten that I am your Rock
and your house is built on me.
You are built on the solid Rock of salvation
which cannot be shaken.

"Therefore everyone who hears
these words of mine
and puts them into practice
is like a wise man
who built his house on the rock.
The rain came down,
the streams rose,
and the winds blew
and beat against that house;
yet it did not fall,
because it had its foundation on
the rock" (MATTHEW 7:24,25).

Wake up and realize where you are.
You are built on me,
your strong, unfailing Rock.
Yes, the storms have come against you,

213

and you feel as if everything
you had hoped for is gone.
But it isn't true.
You need not feel hopeless.

*B*oldly declare as David did:
    "The LORD is my rock,
    my fortress and my deliverer;
    my God is my rock,
    in whom I take refuge,
    my shield
    and the horn of my salvation.
    He is my stronghold,
    my refuge and my savior" (2 SAMUEL 22:2,3).

*A*nother time David said,
    "For in the day of trouble
    he will keep me safe in his dwelling;
    he will hide me in the shelter
    of his tabernacle
    and set me high upon a rock" (PSALM 27:5).

In spite of pressures,
> David knew I was his Rock
> and his place of refuge.
> I am the same for you.

Say with him,
> "In you, O LORD, I have taken refuge;
> let me never be put to shame. . . .
> Be my rock of refuge,
> to which I can always go" (PSALM 71:1,3).

Living Words
of Scripture

He is the Rock, his works are perfect,
> and all his ways are just.
> A faithful God who does no wrong,
> upright and just is he (DEUTERONOMY 32:4).

There is no one holy like the LORD;
> there is no one besides you;
> there is no Rock like our God (1 SAMUEL 2:2).

Who is God besides the LORD?
    And who is the Rock except our
        God? (2 SAMUEL 22:32).

The LORD lives! Praise be to my Rock!
    Exalted be God, the Rock, my
        Savior! (2 SAMUEL 22:47).

Since you are my rock and my fortress,
    for the sake of your name lead and
        guide me (PSALM 31:3).

From the ends of the earth I call to you,
    I call as my heart grows faint;
    lead me to the rock that is higher
        than I (PSALM 61:2).

He alone is my rock and my salvation;
    he is my fortress,
    I will never be shaken (PSALM 62:2).

My salvation and my honor depend on God;
    he is my mighty rock, my refuge (PSALM 62:7).

216

The LORD has become my fortress,
   and my God the rock in whom I take
      refuge (PSALM 94:22).

They drank from the spiritual rock
   that accompanied them,
   and that rock was Christ (1 CORINTHIANS 10:4).

41

I Am the
All-Powerful One

*W*eakened child,
    You have allowed the circumstances
    of your life to make you feel weak as water.
    Indeed, you are powerless
    to change what has happened.
    But you are not powerless
    to change your reaction
    to your circumstances.

*R*emember, I am the All-Powerful One.
    As your God, I can do for you

what you cannot do for yourself.
Recall this truth about me:
"He gives strength to the weary
and increases the power of the
   weak" (ISAIAH 40:29).
Meditate on the fact
of my all-powerful presence
with you at all times.

*D*eclare with the psalmist:
   "You are awesome, O God,
   in your sanctuary;
   the God of Israel gives power
   and strength to his people" (PSALM 68:35).

*Y*ou have permitted yourself
   to develop a spirit of fear.
   Fear is never of me.
   "For God has not given us
   a spirit of fear,
   but of power
   and of love
   and of a sound mind" (2 TIMOTHY 1:7 NKJV).

219

*W*ith the sound mind which I have given you,
     you can be assured that
     "[you] through faith
     are shielded by God's power" (1 PETER 1:5).

*W*hen you feel weak
     and powerless to help yourself,
     recall these words
     and know that they apply to you:
     "His divine power
     has given us everything
     we need for life and godliness
     through our knowledge of him
     who called us by his own glory
     and goodness" (2 PETER 1:3).

*B*ecause I live within you, you can
     relinquish your feelings of weakness
     and "be strong in the Lord
     and in his mighty power" (EPHESIANS 6:10).

Living Words
of Scripture

*B*e exalted, O LORD,
>   in Your own strength!
>   We will sing and praise Your
>   power (PSALM 21:13 NKJV).

I will sing of Your power;
>   yes, I will sing aloud
>   of Your mercy in the morning;
>   for You have been my defense
>   and refuge in the day of my
>   trouble (PSALM 59:16 NKJV).

I have seen you in the sanctuary
>   and beheld your power and your
>   glory (PSALM 63:2).

*S*ay to God, "How awesome are your deeds!
>   So great is your power

that your enemies cringe before
   you" (Psalm 66:3).

*G*od has spoken once,
      twice I have heard this:
      That power belongs to God (Psalm 62:11 NKJV).

*M*ay the God of hope
      fill you with all joy and peace
      as you trust in him,
      so that you may overflow with hope
      by the power of the Holy Spirit (Romans 15:13).

*M*y grace is sufficient for you,
      for my power is made perfect in
         weakness (2 Corinthians 12:9).

*T*o him who is able
      to do immeasurably more
      than all we ask or imagine,
      according to his power
      that is at work within us . . . (Ephesians 3:20).

222

I want to know Christ
and the power of his
resurrection . . . (PHILIPPIANS 3:10).

. . . being strengthened with all power
according to his glorious might
so that you may have great endurance
and patience. . . (COLOSSIANS 1:11).

*Y*ours, O LORD, is the greatness
and the power
and the glory
and the majesty
and the splendor,
for everything in heaven
and earth is yours.
Yours, O LORD, is the kingdom;
you are exalted as head over
all (1 CHRONICLES 29:11).

*T*o him who is able
to keep you from falling

and to present you
before his glorious presence
without fault and with great joy—
to the only God our Savior be glory,
majesty,
power
and authority,
through Jesus Christ our Lord,
before all ages,
now and forevermore! Amen (JUDE 24,25).

42

I Am Your
Ever-Present One

Lonely child of mine,
    I am aware of your loneliness.
    Since your loved one is gone,
    Your heart feels heavy as lead.
    You feel that your pain
    is too much to bear.

I am here to remind you of my presence,
    of my love.
    I never abandon my children.
    Human love often falters,
    but my love for you is sure,

steadfast.
I love you too much to leave you alone.
You are mine,
precious in my sight.

You need not be afraid of being alone,
of being deserted by me.
I am your ever-present Helper,
your Comforter,
the Lover of your soul.

When the darkness settles over the earth
and you feel especially lonely,
remember that I am with you.
I will light your way,
I will be your inner light.

When the dawn spills
into your bedroom window,
reminding you
that another day is before you,
and you feel too crushed to move,

I am your strength.
Lean on me.
I am present to restore you,
to renew your tired body.

When you're not sure of which path to follow,
which decision to make,
I am present.
I will direct you.
Be still and listen for my voice.
I speak softly,
gently.
"Never will I leave you;
never will I forsake you" (HEBREWS 13:5).

Living Words of Scripture

The LORD your God
is the one who goes with you
to fight for you against your enemies
to give you victory (DEUTERONOMY 20:4).

I am convinced
   that neither death nor life,
   neither angels nor demons,
   neither the present nor the future,
   nor any powers,
   neither height nor depth,
   nor anything else in all creation,
   will be able to separate us
   from the love of God
   that is in Christ Jesus our Lord (ROMANS 8:38,39).

I will not in any way fail you
   nor give you up
   nor leave you without support.
   [I will] not,
   [I will] not,
   [I will] not in any degree
   leave you helpless,
   nor forsake nor let [you] down
   (relax my hold on you)!
   [Assuredly not!] (HEBREWS 13:5 AMP).

God is our refuge and strength,
>   an ever-present help in trouble.
>   Therefore we will not fear,
>   though the earth give way
>   and the mountains fall
>   into the heart of the sea . . . .
>   The LORD Almighty is with us (PSALM 46:1,2,7).

In the shelter of your presence
>   you hide them from the intrigues of men;
>   in your dwelling you keep them
>   safe . . . (PSALM 31:20).

Serve the LORD with gladness;
>   come before His presence with
>   singing (PSALM 100:2 NKJV).

Be strong and courageous.
>   Do not be afraid or terrified because of them,
>   for the LORD your God goes with you;
>   he will never leave you nor forsake
>   you (DEUTERONOMY 31:6).

43

I Am Your Rewarder

Dear seeking child,
   Your insecurity causes you
   to look to others for approval and rewards.
   As long as you continue
   expecting rewards from people
   you are likely to be disappointed.
   But I will never disappoint you.

I am your Rewarder.
   "Anyone who comes to [God]
   must believe that he exists

and that he rewards
those who earnestly seek him" (HEBREWS 11:6).

𝒴ou need not always be seeking
approval from others.
You are created in my image,
a creature of dignity in my sight.
I gave my life for you.
Would not I also be the One
to reward you
so that you need not look so often
to others for rewards?

𝒲hen you learn to see yourself from my perspective,
your anxieties about lack of rewards
from others will fade.
You do not doubt my reality
and you are earnestly seeking me.
Therefore you can know of a truth
that I am your rewarder.
"Surely the righteous
still are rewarded" (PSALM 58:11).

231

*P*ut your confidence in me,
     not in others and their opinions.
     You are my beloved child,
     and I want to reward you
     for your faithfulness to me.
     Rely not on the judgments of others,
     but on my promises to you.
     Search my Word for those promises.
     Mark them, lean on them.

I am your Rewarder.

Living Words
of Scripture

*A*fter this, the word of the LORD
     came to Abram in a vision:
     "Do not be afraid, Abram.
     I am your shield,
     your very great reward" (GENESIS 15:1).

*H*e who sows righteousness
     reaps a sure reward (PROVERBS 11:18).

If your enemy is hungry,
>   give him food to eat;
>   if he is thirsty,
>   give him water to drink . . .
>   and the LORD will reward you (PROVERBS 25:21,22).

Surely, O LORD,
>   you bless the righteous;
>   you surround them with your favor
>   as with a shield (PSALM 5:12).

The LORD has dealt with me
>   according to my righteousness;
>   according to the cleanness of my hands
>   he has rewarded me (PSALM 18:20).

Restrain your voice from weeping
>   and your eyes from tears,
>   for your work will be rewarded (JEREMIAH 31:16).

44

I Am Your
Holy One

Growing child,
  You know me as Savior and Friend
  and many other titles.
  I want you to know me as your Holy One,
  and praise me for my holiness
  —not because I need your praise,
  but because praise honors me
  and brings greater peace
  and joy to your life.
  Praise has been called the pathway to peace.

The better you know me as your Holy One,
>the greater will be your ability to praise me.
>"'Do not be afraid . . .
>for I myself will help you,'
>declares the LORD,
>your Redeemer,
>the Holy One of Israel" (ISAIAH 41:14).

When you read,
>"I am the LORD, your God,
>the Holy One of Israel,"
>it also means I am *your* Holy One.
>Indeed, "I am the LORD, your Holy One,
>Israel's Creator, your King" (ISAIAH 43:15).

You may enter into praise
>as my earlier people did:
>"Shout aloud and sing for joy,
>people of Zion,
>for great is the Holy One
>of Israel among you" (ISAIAH 12:6).

My people knew there was reason for joy
   and praise, simply because
   I was the Holy One among them
   Many times you, like they,
   see no reason to praise.
   But they praised me anyway.
   So can you.
   "Once more the humble
   will rejoice in the LORD;
   the needy will rejoice
   in the Holy One of Israel" (ISAIAH 29:19).

You can be blessed as you join them
   in joyfully declaring:
   "I will praise you with the harp
   for your faithfulness, O my God;
   I will sing praise to you with the lyre,
   O Holy One of Israel" (PSALM 71:22).
   Realizing my holiness,
   the psalmist unabashedly
   spoke to his own soul:

"Praise the LORD, O my soul;
all my inmost being,
praise his holy name" (PSALM 103:1).

*H*e then followed through with praise.
You can be blessed as you do the same.

Living Words
of Scripture

"*T*o whom will you compare me?
Or who is my equal?" says the
Holy One (ISAIAH 40:25).

*W*hen they see among them their children,
the work of my hands,
they will keep my name holy;
they will acknowledge the holiness
of the Holy One of Jacob,
and will stand in awe of the God of
Israel (ISAIAH 29:23).

Our Redeemer—the LORD Almighty
        is his name—is the Holy One of
            Israel (ISAIAH 47:4).

This is what the high
        and lofty One says—
        he who lives forever,
        whose name is holy:
        "I live in a high and holy place" (ISAIAH 57:15).

O LORD, are you not from everlasting?
        My God, my Holy One. . . .
        Your eyes are too pure to look on evil;
        you cannot tolerate wrong (HABAKKUK 1:12,13).

Glory in his holy name;
        let the hearts of those
        who seek the LORD rejoice (PSALM 105:3).

Holy, holy, holy is the LORD Almighty;
        the whole earth is full of his glory (ISAIAH 6:3).

My mouth will speak in praise of the LORD.
Let every creature praise
his holy name for ever and ever (PSALM 145:21).

There Is a Balm in Gilead

There is a balm in Gilead
to make the wounded whole.
There is a balm in Gilead
to heal the sinsick soul.
                    —Anonymous